The Male's Guide On How To Avoid Commitment

By The Breakup Guy

Never Buy The Cow

When The Milk Is Free

Relationship consultant—Sagebrush Sandy

Editor—Stacie Smith

(On the cover)

This book is dedicated to

Gary Rowberry

A Riverview Highschool graduate that

Remains single to this day.

Change

Change...it is a very scary thing for a guy. Especially if you are a north county Riverview Guy. Born, bred, and raised in the suburbs of St. Louis, graduating from Riverview Highschool, you have excelled in...just Gym class. Coach Bowen motivated you; he pumped you, worked you, owned you...the Riverview Guy. Coach Bowen was your mentor. Your adviser, counselor and confidante. An ex-marine-sergeant, gone sour, Coach Bowen drilled you for your future. He molded you into a pumping, athletic machine. Being a driven, muscular, apparatus, you, the Riverview Guy proudly surpassed all levels of competition for your coach.

The Riverview Guys. Proud, athletic, very social, yet, reclusive by nature. You possess individual qualities, are very private...yet expressive about your needs. Alas, a dying breed. Confident in most social settings, still awkward at times around the female gender. You, a Riverview Guy...are vocal, moods are expressed in many tones and you are proud of your audio abilities. You howl at the moon. Bodily functions come natural to you. It's your being; your total existence. The absolute keen sense of awareness that you possess, contributes to your very survival. Its in your genes and you wear them well. Total discipline along with your animal instinct, steers you from succumbing to the witch crafts of female persuasion. You are a survivor. And at every family gathering, G.I. Joe from Hasbro was the gift of choice to all your nieces and nephews.

You take pride in the fact that you are single, unattached, successful in business, and confident in all areas of your life. So confident, that you would consider ordering a foo foo drink from a restaurant and bar, but you won't. You, a Riverview Guy, have a high testosterone count.

You talk about it in the locker room. You boast about it at the Super Bowl party; you're healthy, energetic and robust. Handsome, but not gorgeous. Clean, but not tidy. Wholesome, but naughty. Playful by nature, and you proudly live...by the Riverview Code.

The Riverview Code, you ask? Yes, the Riverview Code. The sub-chapter version of The National Male Code. The code that all healthy heterosexual males live by. The Code that rules over all boinking issues. Whether you can rightfully boink or not boink your buddies' ex-wife, ex-girlfriend, ex-roommate, ex-sister-in-law, ex-secretary, ex-dental

hygienist, or ex-bartender at Rich Andrews Saloon. That Code. You know the code, and you know it well.

The code that is unspoken and yet it is honored within many cultural groups of civilized males. Yes, for years, the code has been in effect. True, it is in unwritten form. Never been documented, but yet, it is honored by many. And you, the Riverview Guy...never want to violate the code. No matter how tempting the forbidden fruit has been. Luscious, sweet, and succulent, as it may be, you, will never, violate the code.

You might trespass visually, contrive an illusion of banging your best friend's babe, handcuffed, "doggie style" in a public place...a fantasy beyond your wildest dreams...but you the Riverview Guy, will never the violate the code.

And, just what is the punishment for criminals of sexual misconduct? Code violators are dealt with harshly. To violate the code is profound.

A Riverview Guy knows that the intensity of any affair is never worth the societal rulings of damnation that can take place afterward. Shackled, horsewhipped, then paraded throughout the community for public stoning. (A celebration

before the hanging.) Or being beheaded after a triumphed mockery from the group. Yes, to violate the code could mean life or death in certain cultures. However, for other reasons, the Riverview Guy honors the code. Otherwise, he may be shunned. Boycotted. Eluded in many ways to live out his remainder years with another tribe. Shameless, discredited, ostracized.....and now groping through life, perhaps becoming homeless...all because of one erred boinking. To stimulate the issue even further, a violation of the code must be reported. That's right. *File a report.* As if the situation isn't embarrassing and problematical enough, a Riverview Guy must report the incident, even if the boinking affair did

not actually take place. Whether it involved you or another buddy, having knowledge of the incident or proposal itself, is almost as critical as being the participant. The actual offense of the true and verified offer...along with the method of the approach coming from the babe, has to be reported immediately. The message here is clear. Never violate the code.

WARNING

Current actions are

OUT OF COMPLIANCE

constituting a violation of

written policy on this issue

And to complicate matters, babes don't care. They can be ruthless and brutal. Bawdy, foul and nasty. Down right beastly, ferocious and oh...so cruel. Like calloused, barbaric sharks they are capable of sinking their razor sharp teeth into a male bond, no matter now strong or dynamic it may be. It could be a lifelong friendship, a harmonious connection since pre-school...a rare closeness, nurtured and protected through the years...cherished in the highest esteem...now gone, irreparable, lost forever. Diminished. All

because of a miscalculated boinking. OK, in this case, a blunder boinking. You were tested and you failed. Crashed, slammed and reamed!

Perhaps it was the beer goggles. Or her sweet perfume that weakened your judgement. Maybe it was that she licked her finger tips after eating the BBQ chicken. The truth of the matter is, you lacked in discriminating taste. And betrayal of a Riverview buddy will not be accepted. Zero tolerance here, Pal.

But now, you are faced with a new **dilemma,** that enables you to function like the healthy heterosexual Riverview male, that you, so desire to be. Your daily activities no longer sprint with ease. Sprint, sprint, sprint. You, a Riverview Guy, are not **smooth** anymore. Your eloquent and articulating style is now in the pause mode. Lethargic, dull and inanimate. Perhaps lackadaisical. You no longer feel

macho, cool, alert, and competitive, because...your male existence is being **threatened.** It's a Neanderthal Jeopardy Game at its best. A direct attack coming from the female influence. Your confidence level drops and then, over time...you weaken. Soft and droopy....you are now powerless. And it soon becomes a clothing issue. Your self consciousness is impairing your judgment on your wardrobe. It's critical...it is effecting your style. You are no longer suave and vogue. You were once chic and debonair with a flair. And, now...you cannot decide what to wear. Tommy Hilfiger or Ralph Lauren? Perhaps, just Nike.

You fear, that you are becoming an endangered species. An incredible force that governed your once, cheery, happy mood is now dominating your very soul...deteriorating...crumbling. And the Riverview Guy knows, this could very well be life threatening. You now have **the deer-in-the-headlight-look,** and it's not pretty for the Riverview Guy.

Your heart beats faster, your pulse gets weak, you sweat...you are hyperventilating. You lose your appetite. Yes, you even lose sleep over it. For the first time in your life, you are greatly confused. Totally dazed. The very thought of cohabiting with one woman makes you dizzy. Perhaps, constipated. OK, totally clogged. Oh, why should a man have to deal such issues? Ah, the pressure, of dealing with **commitment.**

First...it happens to a buddy, and now you. Like a fever...it spreads, out of control. It leaves you wondering...how did I allow this to happen to me? How can a woman like that...affect me...a Riverview Guy?

Know this. She...being your girlfriend, masters her strategy by reading books. Know this, books strengthen the female. They cannot function in the male world without having information. And we know, information is power. And females know, information, especially the RIGHT information is their POWER. They read often. And they hide their books in various

locations. Like a squirrel...saving for the future**...(WHICH INVOLVES YOUR FUTURE PAL!)** she buries her strategy. It's on her hard drive too. In hidden files, so cleverly named, in secret directories...that it would take a Private Eye to decipher the total meaning...of...her world to you. It's driving you nutty.

You being the Riverview Guy...are not as strong with your

computer skills, in fact, you are weak. Mastering your sharpshooter technique by Killing The Zombies at Dave & Busters Video Arcade...is your boasted computer skill. You have reason to worry. And worry is not a normal trait for a

Riverview Guy. It's just not pretty.

And the female strategy thing thickens...It's mystifying and baffling to many. Females attend seminars. They like to meet frequently. Surprisingly, there is...no structure to their encounters. It could be scheduled...or it may be spontaneous. It could be for a morning, a day , or even a weekend retreat. Women know how to gather quickly and group if need be. They have the ability to converse in pairs, or talk openly in a very large group in a seminar setting. They can babble about emotional and personal issues with total strangers of the female gender. They can discuss matters in short bursts or in great lengths. It is amazing! This is their strength! They believe in power by numbers. Take heed, as they will involve their mothers, sisters, daughters, cousins, aunts, teachers, neighbors, and even organizations. Know this and know this well, women have a knack for gathering quickly and swiftly.

The Riverview Guy is weak in this area. **You** do not have this skill. You could not plan a meeting or rendezvous if your very life depended on it, unless it evolved around a male macho event such as football. You, hangout with your buddies. This is a security strengthening issue for the Riverview Guy. You bond and you bond often. It's a fact. You connect at clubs and bars, the locker room, sports events and BBQ's. It is never planned. Guys just run into each other. And you...The Riverview Guy being a creature of habit, run into other Riverview Buddies just by doing your routine. Yes, astonishingly as it may seem, the Riverview Guy has a routine. Even if it is not consistent or goal oriented, you have a routine. In fact, you have mastered your professional life very well. It has direction, because you a Riverview Guy, have a business plan. It's your personal life that sucks. And every time it sucks, it sucks for one reason...she's female.

So, while hanging out with your buddies, you talk about issues. It may be in an abrupt tone or it may be very subtle, depending on the occasion. And, depending on the amount of alcohol in your system as well. The issues are sometimes...job related, and some issues may be money related. Many times it is sport related. And once in a while, but not often...the issues will involve females. Generally, you the Riverview Guy are able to avoid all female issues. P.M.S. estrogen, STD and yes...even bloating. You are the master on avoiding female issues...because you are non committal.

But now, this one is staring you in the face...smack, dead, center. Slap, thump and whack!

What ever you do, don't panic. Remaining calm while maintaining your very composure, your style, the coolness that you possess...simply by being a living, breathing Riverview Guy is an absolute necessity. This guide will be your survival plan. It will sustain your life of leisure. After you read this guide thoroughly and live by these rules...you will never a lose a battle on the domestic front again.

First, we will go over the pre-commitment stages of the relationship. I call it insurance. Living by the outlined policy, of macho male standards, will minimize your commitment

attacks. The more skillful you become, the less likely you will become, subjected to attacks of the obligatory nature...directly coming from the enemy, being...the female.

In a powderpuff disguise to portray herself as being refined and gentle, this is the female's best attribute. Some even say she is gifted. Bright and talented. Appearing in the form of innocence and in need of your great strength, she will coo and cry. Females can manipulate tears, lots of tears, weeping in a state

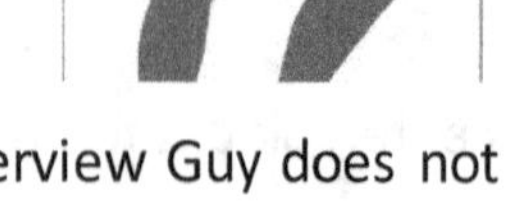

of helplessness. And before you know it, she's turned on you...in less than one minute, she's hissing and clawing like a wildcat. They're bad. Evil and wicked.

To make it even more interesting, a Riverview Guy does not

understand the emotional side of the female. **Hey, Mr. Tin Man!** Yes you, the one without a heart! The only time you shed a tear...is when The Blues Hockey Team loses the Stanley Cup. Or when your best dog runs off. Maybe, when

you horse loses a race...OK Mr. Tin Man? You squeak. And speaking of your ass squeaking when you walk, try some WD 40, it might loosen the cash flow. Babe's don't want the cheap ass economy treatment, either Pal. And...to complicate things even further, they expect you to understand their emotional needs as well!

Right. Like turkeys might fly out of your armpits too. Because we all know there are hundred's of emotional issues when it comes to dealing with females. They cry and they cry often. They cry when fish die. They cry while watching sad movies. They even cry just because it is that time of the month. (Phew!) And that is why you, the Riverview Guy do not care to commit. Think about it. Do you want to be subjected to this very crap day in an day out from this day forward? No Sireee!

The Riverview guy will always want to apply the rules. For your safety and wellbeing, do not violate the rules.

THESE ARE THE RULES:

1) Never display her picture. This is an important issue. Hang posters of super-models, famous babes, but by all means do not place your chick's photo within view. Tuck

it away some where...for masturbating purposes. A drawer, a closet, under your car seat, in the glove box, but never leave it out for public viewing. This will cause her to wonder just how important she is to you. Commitment is definitely out of the question. Now, let's say...she gives you her picture, in a frame. Oh now, isn't that special? And handy too! Obviously, it's ready for hanging or viewing, never the less, it is **conveniently** ready for public viewing. You will have to be extremely clever here. Simply, place the photo next to or behind the dog's photo. This sort of nips this in the bud right there, doesn't it? There is nothing special about having your photo tucked away or placed off to the side with the usual clutter stuff. Chicks like to think they are special to you. That, you are...close...and that she is close to your heart. And chicks know, that guys generally operate out of convenience. Get the picture Pal? By all

means...**DON'T GET THE PICTURE.**

2) Boink often. (This is my favorite rule.) Love City. Passion at its peak. Climax again and again. Bang her morning and night. Tell her you love her and you can't stand to be without her! The mere thought of commitment will never enter her pretty little head. And if you are banging her like a Riverview Guy should, then she won't bring up commitment issues in the first place. So, bang her. Right and left; **boink often**.

3) Monitor Her Time With Girlfriends. Because, without a doubt, women yak. OK, cluck is more like it. Today, a cute chick, tomorrow a clucking hen. They plant ideas into other girlfriends heads, just so they can stir up stuff. They like crisis. They see it on T.V., so therefore they think life isn't normal unless there is a crisis. First they "do lunch." They do lunch often. Women can "do lunch" like they are on death row! "Let's do lunch." They'll meet in the middle of the day at a highly visible and

popular café, picking at their food and clucking. Cluck, cluck, cluck. Chatter, chatter, chatter. And...just who is the topic of conversation, the news item for the day? You are Pal! Front Page News with the female editorial printed along with it. And hundreds of copies are being distributed, right now! Your life is the Hot news Flash...copies being distributed on every corner, right now, as we speak. And it's not the sports page either Howard! Like dirty laundry being aired...your

character...is now tainted. Your soul is trashed. Your personal life is lewd and risqué, not to mention...ruined. Busted. The moral of the story is, drama is at its peak and your life will suffer tremendously because of it. Monitor the babe with intense supervision.

4) Buy her cards of the romantic persuasion, that way you don't have to "think" of silly romantic words that threaten your very manhood. Cards are good. Girls love to receive romantic cards. Even though you didn't write it, she knows that it is a big step on your part, to give a gift from your heart. (Which you know nothing about,

Mr. Tin Man!) Cards are also relatively cheap. (Cheap, is something you do know about!) So, by giving a card of the romantic gesture, you are in essence, protecting your finances too. A friend told me once, "Every time I get involved with a woman, it costs me money." This is true. Quality underwear has costs too, Pal! Go get a "grip" on it. The card thing is buying insurance, and/

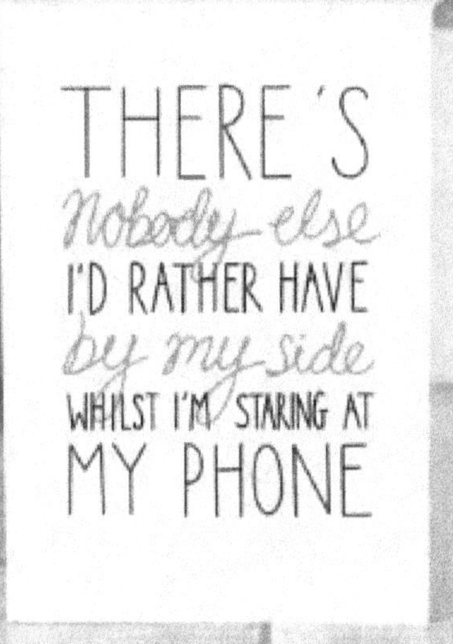

or time in avoiding the commitment thing. I cannot guarantee that the entire process in avoiding commitment will be cheap. No Sir. As we all know, **chicks can be high maintenance.**

5) Never buy her jewelry. What?! Are you breathing?!! This will make your girlfriend, think, that you are committing to the relationship. And jewelry cost money. ($) Jewelry is considered to be the true gift from the heart. Come on! Chicks know this. It is romantic and yet a "stake to your claim." It is **permanent.** Jewelry won't wilt, and it is lasting; a lot of guys fall for this trickery buying into this stuff. However, if your babe is not wearing a ring, then other guys know that she is likely to be fair game. And in a way, she is. So you will have to be careful here. Real careful. Not only are you going to avoid the jewelry

store, but you will have to spend a little extra time keeping tabs on her, the female...because you don't want other heterosexual males preying on your chick! Sniffing her out, like you guys do. Sniff! Sniff!! Sniff!! And, as you know, the babe could be miles away yet, her

alluring presence is SOOO strong, it's frightening. Her silicone breasts are perky, her thighs are trim, and her butt...yeah, she runs a lot, works out too. She's wired, she's ready. She's always ready to boink and it shows. She walks with style. She's fast, she's a mover, she's a tramp..., she's a real seducer. She could seduce your neutered dog! She's hot, she's steamy, she rides so good. She's every cowboy's dream. Yeee hah!!! Sometimes...a little jewelry never hurts.

6) Respect her independence and encourage her to working two jobs. That way, you know where she is at all times. And you have more time to "play" at the gym. Not only are you keeping her busy (and earning her keep), she won't have time to bring up the issue on commitment. Comment often on the fact that you admire her independence. Independent chicks don't' worry about commitment issues.

7) Encourage the Babe To Work Out. You want your babe looking good at all times. You a Riverview Guy,

appreciate a **hard body.** And you cannot compromise by going out with a chick that slacks on her workouts. BE **FIRM** ON THIS.

8) By the way, how is she about oral? It's a workout too you know! Hey! I'm not talking about dental floss here, Pal! Does she do it with a smile? Does she beg for it? It's not about yearning for the Little Debbie Snack Cakes, either! This is your future, Mr. Dweeb! That's right! Because if you are not sure of these things, you might as well get on the Dorkhead Express now. It's your cookies we're talking about here Pal...chocolate chips and all!!!

9) Return all of her items each time she leaves your domain. Pay attention here, this is how women 'mark' their **territory. They** leave 'subtle' hints, she being the female, spends a certain amount of time at your domain. Babes don't hike their leg or flash the wiener like guys do...no sir. They leave little reminders. A clue here...a trace over there. By leaving little chick items at your place, she is reminding you of her presence. If she's a good tramp, it might be panties that were left behind under the sheets, but...if she's a real slut, it's the panties and the bra, hanging from your lampshade. But you, the Riverview Guy know better. You will maintain **control** by gathering up each and every item, toting them to her vehicle, while kissing her goodbye, after each visit. By doing this, she, the female, will think that perhaps she is still being evaluated. Like...you are thinking about it, but you just have not made up your

mind about **HER.** This will surely keep her on her toes. She may even try harder to please you, and yet, she will not fell confident enough to bring up the issues on commitment.

10) Assert yourself in a macho manner by stating early into the relationship that **YOU WILL NEVER MARRY**. This will make her aware of your desires early on. However, you don't' want to waste any time here...with the wrong woman, so you take the initiative and ask her questions. Lots of questions. Pry into her past. **Interrogate** her about her first marriage. Get the really skinny on her. YOU, BEING THE RIVERVIEW GUY THAT YOU ARE, CHOOSE TO BE SELECTIVE ABOUT HIS TIME AND HOW HE SPENDS IT. You want to keep the **offensive** here, and ask this chick more questions. Cross-examine her often. Ask even more questions.

11) Give flowers, so long as they are relatively cheap. ($) A simple rose, or a small bouquet is fine. This is very romantic and she will bubble the very moment you give them to her. Just be sure they are cheap enough. **This should be easy for your Mr. Tin Man.** The more money you spend on her, the more likely she will then detect that she is in fact, important to you and that she has some meaning in your life. Like this could be a serious deal. Once chicks discover this, that is when they start thinking, about future options. And YOU, the Riverview Guy cannot afford to let your girlfriend think along

these lines. NO SIR-EEEE!!!!

12) Take her to "goober" movies early on in the relationship. A good one would be, "The Water Boy",

starring Adam Sandler. That way, she knows up front that you are immature and very boyish with your style. This will deter her very thoughts about long term commitment for a good long while. No hand holding either dude. Hey, another thought...take the dog with you too!!!

13) Take her to remote dinner places. Be sure to take your babe to 'safe" dining places that friends and business associates don't go to. This will keep you from running into influential people. Yes, jughead...important people, that are quite impressive and instrumental to your life...as well as your career...that would otherwise inquire about your date. *Those influential people*. Take her to places that are questionable on paying their utility bills. Dark building, slow running water...you get it.

14) Mind Fuck her. This might seem abrupt or a bit harsh, but this tactic works very well as a preventative measure. Start out by asking her questions about her

orgasms and her INABILITY to having them...as often, that you would like, and...in a timely manner. ("Babe, do you think you can come before my Visa expires?") You, being the River Guy, have the ability to get a hard-on , mount front and center, and you practice keeping it

as well as maintaining it. Longevity, that you are proud of! Asking her in a subtle way about her sexual performance will make her feel very insecure. If necessary, be as so bold to bring up the issue of EMOTIONAL BAGGAGE. A lot of chicks acknowledge this. This tactic will definitely weaken her.

15) Further, point out her sexual dysfunctions, give her something to work on. It is effective. Go ahead, try it. Keep her at this level as long as possible because it is the last preventative measure that a Riverview Guy can use. And this is a survival issue, right guys?

At this point in the game, You the Riverview Guy, should feel a lot better about this. Following through and enforcing the rules will allow you to live and breed by the Riverview

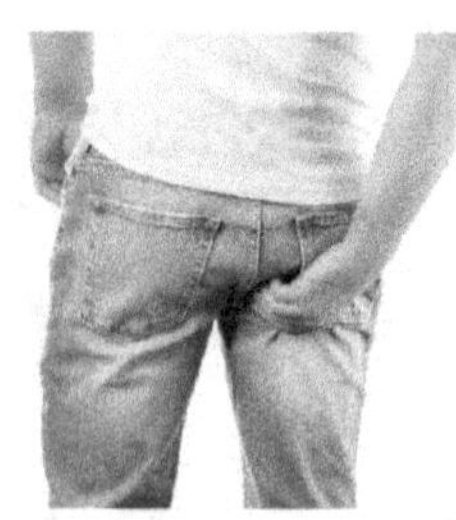

Genetic Code to carry on your genes. The ones that you wear so well. Proud and tall in the saddle. They fit so good. The relaxed fit for long rides. And the slim cut for showing off your cute butt on those boot-scootin'-howling-at-the-moon nights. If there's an itch, you scratch it. If there's a game, you beat it. If there's a target, you shoot it. It is funny what a pair of tight fittin' jeans, on a warm summer night, will do to a Riverview Guy just to impress a female.

But, we all know, that without warning, things can get out of hand and erupt into the next phase. **Yes, the next phase.** Like volcanic lava, seething...steaming...bubbling...never ending...this is a very delicate and volatile phase. This is the critical and painful growing phase that determines, where you are actually going with it. **(With what?)** Time is growing short. ("I'm sorry, what did you say, babe?") And a new tactic has come into play. ("Babe, could you repeat the question? I'm not sure I understand the question.") It is called...the direct approach. And females are very good with the direct approach. Once your relationship gets to this point. YOU THE RIVERVEW GUY will have to be very creative. So, you will have to keep the evasive, not so direct approach. Especially if you want to keep her around. OK. YOU KNOW IN YOUR HEART, that you do want to keep her around. You just have not figured out a way...as to **HOW** you were going to keep her around. So far, you are doing real well with this.

Pay attention, for every question...she, the female asks you, you simply pretend that YOU THE RIVERVIEW GUY, do not hear her. When she the female repeats the question, then you of course, DO NOT UNDERSTAND THE QUESTIONS. **(GAME SHOW ROUND—GOING FOR POINTS!)** Play this one out...it is a great stalling tactic. It will buy you time. After all, YOU THE RIVERVIEW GUY has taken pride in his Neanderthal ways, by **NOT EVER PLANNING A DOMESTIC MOVE IN HIS ENTIRE LIFE.**

A "domestic move" to the Riverview Guy, is deciding which sofa to lay on during the football game. Domestic decisions to the Riverview Guy, is deciding if you want the "babe" to come over during the game and perhaps have her wait on you. Beer, cuddle, head. In that order. But we all know that chicks have a different idea as to what "domestic move" means. For some reason, they, being females believe that you two are to live together. And once that happens, it is over. **(WHAT??? ARE YOU BREATHING???) DONE. PUT A FORK IN IT MISTER. PULL THE TRIGGER NOW!** So, knowing this, will tell YOU THE RIVERVIEW GUY, that this indeed, is a touchy

and temperamental phase to be in. Things could blow at anytime. Explode. Kabowie, Kabam!

For this reason, you will want to "feel" her out on a daily basis. Mentally! Actually, an hourly basis would not be such a bad idea. Approach her with caution. **EXTREME CAUTION.** Nonchalantly ask her if she had taken her calming pills that morning. Greet her with a hug and a kiss by saying , "Hi Babe-I-Tude!" Search her facial expressions. Study her mannerisms. How does she look to you? Sweet, cuddly, innocent? Stare deep into her bedroom eyes...are they alluring, soft and gentle? Or...perhaps, there are daggers ready to soar from her very pupils, to ambush your heart? Looks can be so deceiving with babes. Especially older and more wiser ones. You could have swore her breasts were

more fuller just the day before. (Ah, the underwire pushup bra.)

Chicks have the ability to dress any part that they care to be. One day, they pretend they are a sensuous Website Goddess, and the next, they are a Pentecostal Princess. They can be blonde one day and brunette the next. This is why, you the Riverview Guy have to check on your babe and find out just which part she is playing that day.

For added insurance, screw up often. Go out with your Riverview buddies and get drunk. Trashed. Howl at the moon! Drive for long hours. Don't tell her where you are. Just do it. Drive for miles and miles to a low-life bar in another state and get tanked. **Aquarium City, Pal!** Make her think that you are not worth it. Make her doubt that you are the most wonderful thing that ever happened to her. Convince her you have no direction in your life and that you are so disconcerting on the domestic front. This tactic will definitely create doubt.

On to the next mind trap. Suggest that SHE, see a therapist. Chicks are big on therapy. They believe in open communication with their boyfriends, spouses and significant others, so long as they are GETTING THEIR OWN WAY ABOUT THE ISSUES. Send her to the therapist once a week, and have her file a report with you. That way, you will know EXACTLY what's on her mind.

Don't stop now, Pal. Tell her that your old girlfriend called and left a message saying, she is still in love with you. This will definitely make your current (because nothing lasts forever, Pal) babe feel confident. In fact, this will encourage your chick, to please you to no end. She will worry herself to a frazzle, wondering if you are ACTUALLY thinking...of going back with your old girlfriend that she...the current babe will TRY HARDER! Trust me, she, the female, will not bring up commitment when another babe is chasing you.

At times, it may get rough. A little bumpy, and more intense...that you may have to resort to pretending that you are Gay. **That's right, Fag City, "drive-me-home pappa...all the way down the Hershey Highway", gay!** OK, I know this is not easy for a Riverview Guy. I mean, we're talking about a man, a sexual driven man...that lives to boink chicks! To exercise his bodily functions in a competitive form. It's a quest, for the Riverview Guy, to see how long he can keep it up with his chick and how many times he can cum. It's a testosterone journey on penile erection. A crusade for spewing large quantities of cum. This is what the Riverview Guy lives for!

We're talking serious play here. **WHAT ARE YOU BREATHING?** The Riverview Guy wakes up "ready to play." The Riverview Guy is always on "Boink Alert." He is always looking for signs, no matter how subtle or direct they may be. The Riverview Guy is aware of the right time and place to boink. He knows it can happen at any given time. The Riverview Guy is...penile programmed!

That's right. It's in your blood, the signals connect from your brain to all your manly body parts. You know dang well when it is time to perform.

You, the Riverview Guy are well aware of the boinking signs. **Yes, the signs:**

The eye contact. Pronounced, yet so elusive. The sparkles

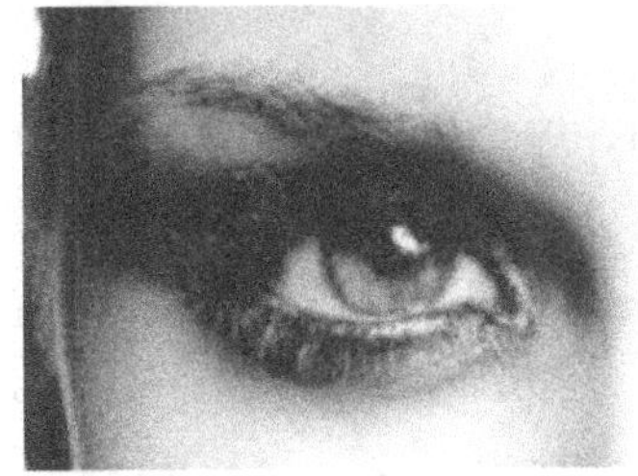

that dance around her, the female. The song...the three piece horny band that follows her, and the spring in her airy, yet, confident step. Her nails are done, her hair is wild and her lipstick spells trouble.

She's dressed to kill. Her perky breasts are peaking for attention. You look...she caught you looking...you turn away. The cautious, quick glance...you immediately identify and acknowledge the target.

She's aloof, remote and hot...like a desert island. Yet convenient, like a drive thru tramp. She's on a mission... a quest, to conquer the male spirit. And she's hungry...for meat. And now, she's going to eat off of the love plate...slowly chewing and devouring every bite. And what's for dinner? **YOU ARE PAL!** Because you, the Riverview Guy have **heterosexual** stamped on his forehead, in **bold** print!

So maybe the gay thing might be a dead giveaway to your intent. And a Riverview Guy is suppose to be good at hiding his intent, as well as hiding his true feelings. So, perhaps you may want to merely, behave a little on the bi-sexual side. Meaning...you could hump a fence post in a heartbeat, if need be.

You see, sometimes, being a Riverview Guy along with having a keen sense of awareness to your penile functions will get you in trouble. This is why it makes it easy, for the female to move in for the kill. To make matters worse, the Riverview guy knows that he is weak to the female influence. Yes, you are aware that, you can fall prey at any given time to the trained female, a true professional. The "seasoned" female is very capable of trapping her male

victim just for sheer pleasure.   Hear the chant buddy, because she's coming after you, Pal!

She'll taste you, lick you...nibble her way to your heart;

She'll suck you, drain you...then tear you apart.

She's a class act...a temptress and a sleaze;

A true heartbreaker, so willing to please.

She'll ride you hard and put you away wet;

Looking as smooth as silk...while playing hard to get.

She's a wild cat...a seductress and a tease;

She purrs at the sign of danger in the midnight breeze.

She's trouble alright...a sorcerer on the go;

Enticing you with laughter, bewitching to your very soul.

She'll torment you, haunt you...and make you her slave; Pretending all along, "it's you that I crave."

Next, she'll drop you in a heartbeat, for somebody new...she's ready for a new game...it's just not with you.

This is why the entire female issue is perplexing to you, the Riverview Guy, because...your physical needs are in the high maintenance category Pal. This is why you are weak in this area. You need it and you need it bad. You gotta have it, but you don't want to pay for it either. The Riverview guy likes cheap women. And sometimes, as perplexing as it is...it cost a lot of money to look cheap too, Pal! Hasn't Dolly taught you anything? Hello!!!! Buying the cow, is not a policy of the Riverview Guy. Free milk is.

And to find good pussy...you have to find the milk.

Sometimes, you are so stressed out about all these issues, that it make you crazy. Dizzy. It impairs your ability to think even though thinking is not a regular routine for the Riverview Guy with a Neanderthal past. Your instincts are all wrong. You can't concentrate. All because of a matter called penile overload. That's right. The dreaded, clogged pecker. A pecker that won't cooperate and run efficiently is aggravating. Because a happy pecker is always working and working efficiently. And we all know his job is...grinding. And so far, the only thing getting the grind around her Pal, is the coffee! It's nerve wracking to the point, that you couldn't find pussy in a cat box on the East Side! You, the Riverview Guy cannot tolerate this pressing matter. You will simply have to address this issue at once. Because now...you are no longer easy to deal with and your Riverview buddies are aware of this. You are about to be moved down on the friendship scale Pal, if you don't do something quick. You will be put on probation until further notice so you need to do something now!

Masturbate. Don't delay. Just do it. The pressure has to be relieved. That's right. Stroke the chicken, spank the monkey, flog the bishop, what ever you want to call it, just do it! Got it Howard?? Or you won't be able to see straight...and you have to finish this manual soon.

Feel better? I told you so! OK, where were we...heart, finances, survival. Oh yeah.

Remember, you're protecting you finances as well as your heart. And females are quick to recite their "no deposit, no return" policy to you, once your penis has traveled beyond the vaginal wall. Remember that. Because of this, sometimes by being a Riverview Guy, means you have to go to the extreme to protecting your sauna. No matter how extreme these methods may seem, you can rest assure that these are proven techniques to avoiding commitment.

In the proper Riverview from, tell her...you are not sure if she in fact, does want to spend time with you. Plant the seed of doubt here. You want proof! Absolute proof that she wants you. Not 75 proof either, 100% proof. You need evidence! You have the right to know! Let her know that you have a gut feeling about something...you just don't know exactly what, for now. Whatever you do, under no circumstances should you let on that you are scared. Down right fearful. Shaking in your boots, scared. That's right. The mere thought of even discussing commitment issues with you chick is a big step on your part. However, just by discussing the very topic is considered

breaking a rule for the Riverview Guy. And, you are taking a risk. A big risk. It's called...being expelled from the group. That's right, we're talking suspension here Pal!

For this reason you want to adopt the following behavior patterns:

1. **Avoid the real issues.** That's right. Side-step. Dance around the issues. Politicians know this technique real well, and it works!!! So far, you are having a real good time with your chick...and then one day, wham!!! The tables turn. First, she is planning a night out, then...a weekend...your super bowl party...next, it will be your life!!! If you allow this to happen, your life is over as we know it. And I mean, tombstone ready. Your epitaph will read "He was a super Riverview Guy." So, if you're letting

this happen to you buddy...just bite the big hook big time. Go ahead. Bite it. Drop you head back and open your mouth real wide...GO AHEAD, TAKE THE BAIT! Because that is exactly what she, the female will do if

you don't avoid the real issues—now.

You see, you're being played, Pal. Like a piano. In style on a Baby Grand. Ivory keys and all. She'll even ask you...with the sweetest smile, "Babe what would you like to hear?" She'll whisper it with her dreamy, luscious, wet lips...while wearing the right shade. Pink fantasy. And her fantasy...is now becoming YOUR NIGHTMARE!!!

Come on, snap out of it! Wake up and smell the coffee!!! Because you, the Riverview Guy are about to become a big time loser...**AND TIME IS RUNNING OUT, PAL!**

2. As a Riverview Guy, you will have to learn how to **divert away from the issue.** Attorneys are real good at this. Simply put it in another perspective for her. (a.k.a. pointing blame in another direction.) Let's say your babe has just accused you of avoiding the issues and being non-committal. Tell her she has been emotional and changes direction too often. (Right Pal, like what does that have to do with the price of eggs in China? And who gives a shit if their chickens are happy, sitting

under warm, cheery, lamps in an energy controlled environment?) This technique, will divert her attention momentarily. Especially if she is blonde. However, if this does not work...you, **YES, YOU...THE RIVERVIEW GUY...WILL HAVE TO BE PREPARED FOR THE INEVITABLE … OF BEING EXPELLED BY THE RIVERVIEW BOYS.**

That's right. As if ridicule isn't bad enough. The very thought of being expelled is total humiliation. Hey, we're not talking probation here Pal! Not a simple revocation matter either! No Sireee. Total suspension!! Because...your case has been monitored from the VERY night of your first date with this babe. Little did you know...that you, The Riverview Guy, has been tested by the boys all along. They have a file on you with a 10 page evaluation attached. THEY KNOW...YES...THEY KNOW, you have this chick. You and her have been spotted in public, because you slipped up. You took her out to a public eating establishment where associates and friends sometimes meet. You probably weren't even aware that you were seen. Caught on video....but you were. A simple, innocent outing to Blockbuster Video to plan your evening just the two of you, can turn into a night of boink media alert with your Riverview buddies. This leads to judicial humiliation. This type of ridicule can be the ruin of a Riverview Guy. This could mean, tragedy. A total disaster! If this happens, it's quite simple. **YOU'RE DEAD. FORGET IT.**

They know , you know, everyone just knows. They

know...you're boinking! Even though you were careful to avoid. P.D.A. (public display of affection.) It's over! There is no back tracking...you cannot cover your tracks once you are boinking on a regular basis, along with being spotted in public! The boinking cloud just hovers over your head the entire time! (Hello?!!! this spells relationship!)

OK. You've been caught at the boinking game.

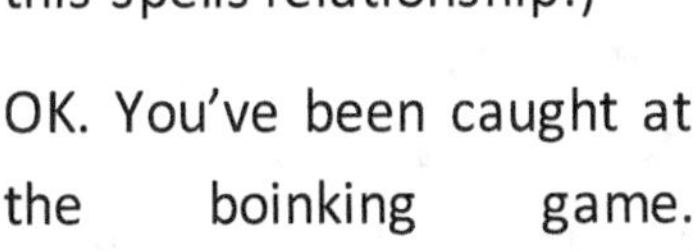

Everyone knows. Your friends, your family, co-workers...even the dog knows. Actually, the dog knew for a long time. The dog was there the first time you boinked the babe! What??? Are You Breathing? I'll give you some hints. While wagging his tail, excess drool, sniff, sniff...he smells the sheets afterward. Are you with me Pal?!

To make matters worse, the dog digs your chick too! YOUR dog digs this chick so much, that he no longer pays any attention to you. And NOW, you are having discipline problems. All because you started boinking this chick. And the little voice goes off in your head, **"DROP DOWN AND GIVE ME 20 NOW, BUD! YOU ARE WORTHLESS AND WEAK!"**

You a Riverview Guy are starting to weaken. Your self-esteem is suffering. And you are thinking that perhaps your career may even be questionable at this point. You are now doubting everything. All because you did not follow the rules. You are so weak, you are even considering a future with this babe. Whatever you do, evaluate the situation, quickly and thoroughly...namely, HER, THE FEMALE.

First, let's look at this from a different perspective. Let's just say, she, the female has found a place in your heart. But you, a Riverview Guy knows that he can take her or leave her.

OK, let's just say that you miss her when she's gone, but only when she's gone. But not a lot, because you the Riverview Guy can deal with this. After all, you were an only child, totally immersed, self centered...never had to share your toys when you were little...and you had the whole playground to yourself. Well, **RECESS IS OVER, PAL!!! THE GAME HAS ENDED. YOUR LIFE IS ABOUT TO COME TO A SCREECHING HALT IF YOU DON'T DO SOMETHING ABOUT IT NOW. WE'RE TALKING EMERGENCY DOMESTIC ACTION.** This is your last chance to avoid commitment.

More rules and domestic warnings:

1. NEVER GIVE EVER GIVE HER THE KEY TO YOUR APARTMENT. If you break this rule, you are giving the babe, a direct invitation to invading your space. You know, your castle. Your enchanted world. The very

castle that you are King of. THINK ABOUT IT. Little domestic items just magically start to appear on the home front. Like domestic wizardry. Cutesy kitchen towels, bathroom toiletries, pictures…(AND YOU CAN GUARANTEE, IT'S A PICTURE OF HER, POSING WITH YOUR DOG.) These items instantly pop up, out of nowhere. You could have sworn that you lived here. And, you pay the rent, right? Of course, you do, Mr. Business Man! You're paying for everything!!! Mortgage/rent, utilities, car, pet bills (on a dog that no longer listens to you) yard work, dinner, groceries, light bulbs…they add up too, you know!

2. Closet space? FORGET IT PAL! Her clothes are multiplying as we speak. Go on, check it out. The hall closet gets taken over first. It's a jacket, a couple of workout suits. The bathroom closet…and then, poof! Where did YOUR work shirts go? Try the rear closet, behind the shelf. Testosterone no longer rules in your castle bud. Cut and dry, guy. Listen up Pal, estrogen rules…in your domain, your castle, right now.

3. Then there's the romantic crap. Foo Foo chick stuff shows up all over the place. The scented candles, her favorite wine…Michael Bolton cd's. **HEY! LISTEN UP DUDE! A RIVERVIEW GUY DOES NOT ALLOW CANDLES, CHICK WINE AND BABE-I-TUDE MUSIC IN HIS DOMAIN.** NO SIR. A Riverview Guy is selective about this stuff! Roller blades, football jerseys, sweats, running shoes, hockey stick…it all has it's own space in the bedroom!

Not to mention your dumbbells that are laying around on the living room floor.

4. But, let's just say, your babe is a little jock. She plays hard, too. She's a serious competitor. Figure skating, soccer and don't forget the equestrian stuff too. (All babes like the horsey stuff.) In addition to your SELECTIVE STUFF being properly stored in your apartment, I mean castle, now SHE, the female has elected to "store" her athletic things right along with your stuff. Well now, isn't that special??!! Her shit, is NOW...mixed up with your shit!

It's an easy mistake to make. Most guys give out their key the babe, thinking...instant pussy. Like you can whip it up in 20 seconds or less. The 24 hour convenient store item. Guys like the idea of living with immediate, access to pussy. Yeah, right Pal! The only immediate access you have to pussy now, is the cat. Her Cat! The one that moved in along with her, the female.

- **C**at - **C**rowded apartment

- **C**astle - **C**ommitment.

- **C** how that works?

- *NEVER, NEVER GIVE OUT THE KEY.*

One more point. Once you start living together...cohabiting...shack up...room together...what ever you call it...the sex stops. No more quickies. Bye Bye good sex. No pussy. It just stops. **THE ONLY THING GETTING LAID AROUND HERE PAL, IS THE CARPET!**

The NEW carpet that you paid for that was her idea in the first place!   Way to go pal.

5.   THE ADDED INSURANCE RULE: CLUTTER YOUR APARTMENT, I MEAN CASTLE, LIKE A HIGH-SCHOOL JOCK.

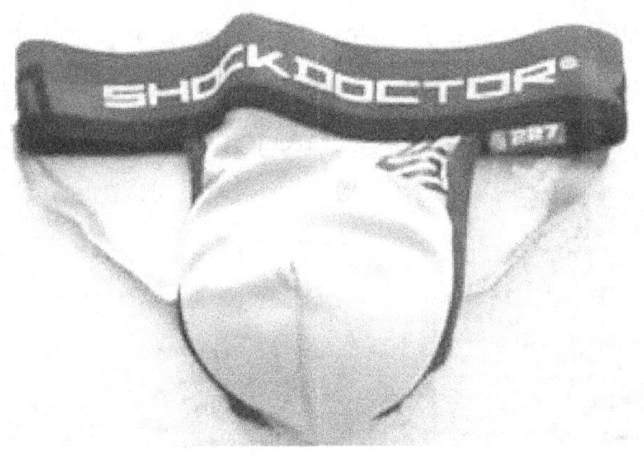

That's right. Keep your athletic equipment within view at all times. Lay everything out on the floor. Basketball, baseball equipment, football, gym clothes, jerseys, golf clubs, and don't forget your jockstrap either. Oh hey, your saddle too! This is a little added athletic touch that you carried over since your high-school and rodeo days. This sends a clear message to your chick that you are still a boy and that you don't intend to grow up...ever. And boys, are not able to commit. Right? Leave piles of sweaty gym clothes on the floor. You know the sequence. The first pile is mildly worn, and can be used again. The second pile has been worn...and requires the sniff test prior to wearing again. And, the third pile... baked to perfect...ready for the laundry room. Any questions? That is what I call the clutter plan. No babe wants to pickup after her guy, day in and day out. Commitment? ("Commit to what babe? To pick up my laundry? Sure, doll!") OK, I think you get it.

6. NEVER INCLUDE HER INTO YOUR PLANS. NO. DEFINITELY NOT. You do your deal, and she does hers. If you start, letting the "Babe-I-Tude' run with you, then it's like you are joined at the hip. And you and the babe should be joined at the hip for one reason only. Boink City. With a capital B. If you let the babe run with you, then it's over Pal. No more freedom. And a Riverview Guy is very much free and independent. Like the wind. You don't want your independence to turn into a summer breeze, do you? A little whirl of Babe-I-Tude bliss can ruin the entire show here. So, let's be smart about this, OK guys? *Don't let the babe run with you.*

7. PROLONG FAMILY INTRODUCTIONS. The moment you introduce the babe to the family, you're inviting trouble. Especially if Mom or Aunt Dot get a hold of her. They're going to want to know every bit of the goods on her! One family dinner...and it can ruin the entire setup, Pal. Now... all the females in your family will want to know if you two are having future plans... (commitment!) *Keep the babe away from your family.*

By the same token, you don't want to meet her family either. No Sir! Maybe her brother...if he plays pro-football. If he plays pro-football or pro-hockey. That couldn't hurt. Front row tickets, box seats...season pass, hey! The brother is cool, it's the rest of the family that sucks.

8. NEVER INTRODUCE YOUR CHICK TO CO-WORKERS. Once you have made this professional introduction, the game is over. Remember the cute little receptionist that has a crush on you? This error of introduction will stifle that for sure. Extinguished. No more spark. The fire is gone. She, the female (the one you are boinking night and day) will be calling you at work, to say cute little nothings, like ... "I can't wait to get ahold of you...to kiss on you, I sure do miss you!" She'll now be calling in the morning, after lunch, before you leave...just to say, "I love you." And, a Riverview Guy has his professional life in order. Remember? (It's your personal life that is a sheer mess, and you want to keep it that way!) Keeping her away from the work place will for sure guarantee that you are commitment free.

9. KEEP A HECTIC SCHEDULE. That's right, stay busy. Work long hours and cram in extra activities after work. Say, like...working out. Or...meeting business associates for a drink, after office hours. By doing this, you will have less time for your chick. You don't want to be too generous with you time, or you might fall into the intimacy trap. **Yes, the intimacy trap.** Chicks are real big on using the word "intimate." It sounds so sensual. Like you and she

have bonded. (!!!!!!) First, it starts out that you're having a good time, sex is great and you're talking...sharing...(there's another chick word) and then wham-o! You are now placed in the intimate category. **It's a trap, Pal! And you're in it!** Snap!! Once again, your heart has been ambushed. Another chick attack on your emotional psyche, that you...the Riverview Guy, so very well, kept hidden...protected...until now. Walk away from this buddy, run if you have to, (faster!) Keeping a hectic schedule (or pretending that you have one) will help you to avoid commitment.

10. Call her. Call her, let's say, maybe twice a day. The morning is a good time to start. This is nothing more than quick chick check. By calling her, you can determine what kind of mood your babe is in. Chicks are moody. 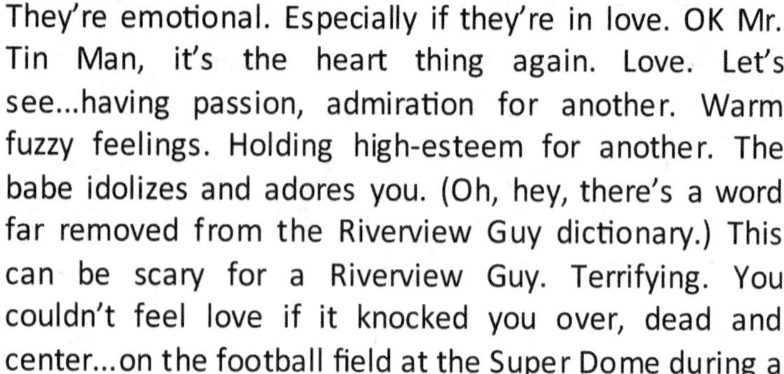
They're emotional. Especially if they're in love. OK Mr. Tin Man, it's the heart thing again. Love. Let's see...having passion, admiration for another. Warm fuzzy feelings. Holding high-esteem for another. The babe idolizes and adores you. (Oh, hey, there's a word far removed from the Riverview Guy dictionary.) This can be scary for a Riverview Guy. Terrifying. You couldn't feel love if it knocked you over, dead and center...on the football field at the Super Dome during a touch down! **What are you breathing?** That is why you answer to Mr. Tin Man. You've been to see the wizard alright. After 6 shots of tequila and 8 beers, you leaned over to the old man on your right and asked, "where can I get a heart?" and the old man replied, "If you must fart, please go to the men's room." You've been lost ever since Pal!

And...the scarecrow hanging with that walking piece of carpet that has been looking for courage...has found it bigtime along with you, in a Bud-Light bottle.

Heart? It's more like lust. The lingering thirst for juicy sex. And it is never quenched! Your desire is too strong. You, the Riverview Guy are penile programmed. You're in love all right, Pal! For ten minutes on a good day, when the weenie is ERECT and saluting! So tell her you love her and miss her, but don't commit your day or any part of it, until it fits in with your entire schedule.

(What schedule, you ask?) The Riverview Guy agenda that has been adopted after the Neanderthal Man's Schedule. That schedule, bozo!

The chick check will keep you apprized of any possible estrogen moments that may be brewing. Yes, estrogen moments. Steaming, simmering, then to a boil and before you knew it was coming...the major cat fight.

(Mee— eeee——o——w!!! Then the tears. That estrogen moment. The chick check will help you to avoid all this

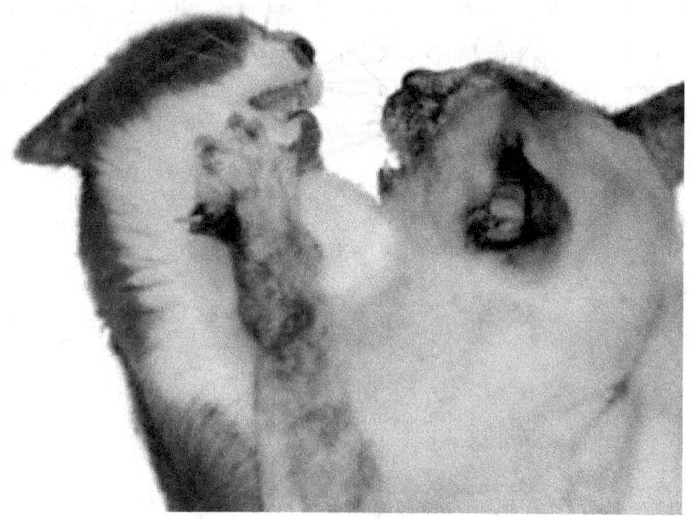

unnecessary, teary, chick stuff. So, let's practice, ok guy? Ready?"

Hi babe!!!! I miss you!!! I sure do love you!!!!" (Pause...) "Really? Oh...gotta go hon, my appointment is waiting, yeah..., I will call you later!" **(MUCH LATER.)** Obviously boinking is not in the Riverview Guys schedule after receiving bad karma from a routine chick check. This is where, you, The Riverview Guy is now aware that you could easily become a target. BULLS-EYE! Turn off your cell phone, leave your pager in the car. This is where you will want to take a temporary leave of absence.

A Riverview Guy is good at taking a temporary leave of absence. This is not to be confused with the Missing In Action plan, where you are gone for days at a time, simply because you were having more fun than what humans are allowed to have. No. This is an absence that may be noted or..., it may not be noted. Depending on how short your leash is. Yes, the leash, the one that jerks you right back when you try to wander, whether it is your boots that were

made for walking or the eyeball that cannot be harnessed. Are you getting it chum?!!! **Disappear! Fade into the night. VANISH. YOU'RE GONE**. Like an abandoned website with no address. No one knows where you are. **CHICK CHECK**. Make it your daily routine.

There you have it. Proven techniques on how to avoid commitment. Vital information on how to remain a single and care free guy. Expertise that you will pass down to your offspring, should you have any. The superior skills, that enhanced the Neanderthal man's way of living, that your grandfather passed onto you. (Surprisingly, sometimes it skips a generation.)

Now, you can sprint and play hard...remain your cool and reflective self...collected and composed...crisp and deliberate like your morning cereal. Aloof, arrogant at times...and charming. Sometimes cosmopolitan. Fresh and delightful. Amusing and perhaps even, delectable. Oh yes, the enchanting you is back. The sparkle in your eyes, that nectarous smile. You are precise and right on the money with your wardrobe...It's you babe...You're back and you have the look. (What look you ask?) That feisty and gallant "do" that you styled yourself. Uhm. Uhm. Uhm. Flat out gorgeous...dazzling...so sexy, and simply marvelous. Just what babes will kill for...

CONFIDENTIAL DATA
PROTECTED
CONFIDENTIAL DATA

Gary Rowberry, Riverview Highschool Graduate
Still single to this day.

"I'm Gary Rowberry and I approve this message."